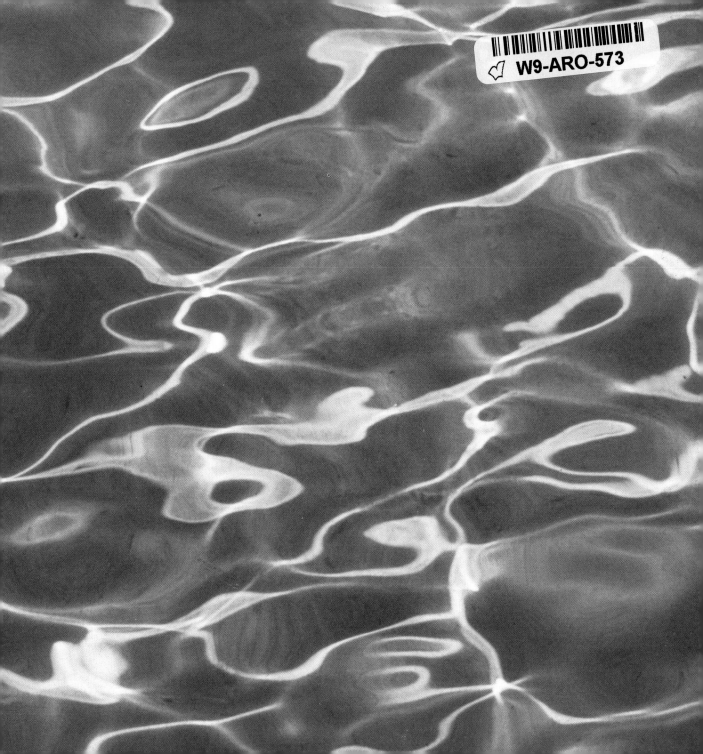

A DK Publishing Book

Text Christopher Maynard
Project Editor Caroline Bingham
Art Editor Claire Penny
Deputy Managing Art Editor Jane Horne
Deputy Managing Editor Mary Ling
Production Ruth Cobb
Consultant Theresa Greenaway
Picture Researcher Tom Worsley

Additional photography by Max Gibbs, Steve Gorton, Frank Greenaway, Dave King, Susannah Price, Pete Gardner, Tim Ridley, David Rudkin, Clive Streeter, Philip Dowell

First American Edition, 1997
2 4 6 8 10 9 7 5 3 1
Published in the United States by DK Publishing, Inc.,
95 Madison Avenue, New York, New York 10016
Visit us on the World Wide Web at http://www.dk.com

Published in Great Britain by Dorling Kindersley Ltd.

A CIP catalog record for this book is available from the Library of Congress.

ISBN: 0-7894-1531-3

Color reproduction by Chromagraphics, Singapore
Printed and bound in Italy by L.E.G.O.

The publisher would like to thank the following for their kind permission to reproduce their photographs:
t top, b bottom, l left, r right, c center, BC back cover, FC front cover
Bruce Coleman Collection: Nick de Vore (Why are there waves?)bl, (Why don't camels...?)c; **James Davis**: (Why does water freeze?)c; **The Image Bank**: G Brimacombe (Why does water turn to steam?)c; **Images Colour Library**: (Why do pebbles...?)cr, (Why do I sweat...?)tr, (Why can't I breathe underwater?)cl; **The National Trust**: Ian Shaw (Why is water like a mirror?)tr; **Pictor International**: (Why do pebbles...?)c; **Rex Features**: (Why do pebbles...?)bl; **Tony Stone Images**: (Why can't I breathe underwater?)c, BC cb, Lori Adamski Peek (Why do I sweat...?)c, Martin Barraud (Why are there waves?)br, John Lawrence (Why is water like a mirror?)c, Dennis O'Clair (Why can't I breathe underwater?)tr, James Randklev (Why does water turn to steam?)br. World Perspectives (Why are there waves?)cr; **Telegraph Colour Library**: FC cb, (Why are there waves?)c, Endpapers

Questions

Why is water like a mirror?

Why does water turn to steam?

Why does water freeze?

Why do pebbles make ripples?

Why are there waves?

Why do I sweat when I run?

Why don't camels need to drink everyday?

Why can't I breathe underwater?

WHY
are there waves?

Questions children ask about water

DK

All objects reflect light into our eyes so we can see them. When sunlight is reflected off trees onto a still lake, the light rays bounce off the water, producing a clear image like a mirror does.

Why do we need water?
Water is the main ingredien of plants and animals – you body is about 60% water.

mirror?

Why do rivers always flow the same way?
Since water can't run uphill, every single river in the world must flow downhill toward the lowest place it can find – the ocean.

Without water plants soon wilt and die, and so would you. Each day your body loses about a half gallon (2.5 liters) of water, so you need to replenish the supply regularly.

Water is made up of particles called molecules. When you heat water, the molecules begin to move around. The hotter it gets, the faster they move – some even escape into the air, or vaporize, as hot steam.

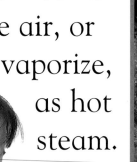

Why does glass steam up?
When warm, moist air hits cold glass, it cools down quickly. The vaporized water

turn to steam?

Why does boiling water bubble?

If water is heated to 212°F (100°C), it starts to turn into steam. This happens so fast on the heated bottom of a pan that the steam makes a trail of bubbles as it rises through the water.

urns back into liquid water,
orming mist on the glass.
Try breathing on a cold mirror
and you'll see this for yourself.

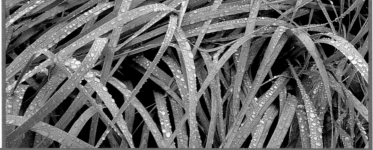

Why does water

If water cools to 32°F (0°C), the tiny molecules that make it up slow down so much that they stick together and the water turns solid. Solid water is called ice.

Why don't fish freeze in icy water?
Ice is lighter than water and it floats to the surface of a freezing pond. The water

freeze?

Why is ice sticky?
Really cold ice cubes
can freeze the thin
layer of moisture
on your fingertips
as you touch them.
For a sticky
instant, you
and the cubes
are frozen
together!

below stays several
degrees warmer, and
that's just right for
a freshwater fish.

Each ripple you see on a pond when you drop a pebble is a tiny wave, set off by the impact of the pebble hitting the water. Ripples happen because water is a liquid.

Why do rivers flood?
When snow melts, or after heavy storms, water

make ripples?

Why are rivers so curvy?
If land was smooth, rivers would run downhill in straight lines. But land is bumpy, with rocks and hills, so rivers wind around to find the easiest path to the ocean.

can pour into a river much faster than the river can carry it away. The water level rises, and may burst over the riverbanks and flood the land nearby.

Waves are made by the wind. When wind brushes over water, it pushes it up into little waves. When it is very windy, the little waves pile up and can grow as big as hills.

Why is seawater so salty?
Rivers collect sediment and minerals, like salt, and deposit them in the ocean.

waves?

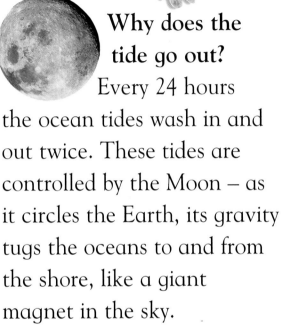

Why does the tide go out?
Every 24 hours the ocean tides wash in and out twice. These tides are controlled by the Moon – as it circles the Earth, its gravity tugs the oceans to and from the shore, like a giant magnet in the sky.

he seawater then evaporates, eaving the salt behind. Thus, ver millions of years, the water as become more and more salty.

Why do I sweat

When you get hot, tiny glands in your skin leak drops of salty water. These quickly evaporate, cooling you down by removing heat.

Why does my skin wrinkle in the tub?
Spend a while in the water and the top layers of your skin begin to soak it up. As they do, they swell, like a grain of rice, and become wrinkled and bumpy.

when I run?

Why does my mouth water?
When your brain knows it's time to eat, it tells your mouth to get ready by making lots of watery saliva to help you chew, and start the digestion process.

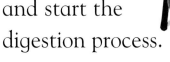

Why don't camels neec

A camel has a huge stomach, and it can drink about 30 gallons (114 l) of water at once. A camel is good at conserving water, too – it can go up to 10 months without a drink.

Why can some creatures walk on water?
The particles of water attract each other, so particles on the

o drink everyday?

Why doesn't a cactus plant need much water?
A cactus can go for weeks without rain by storing water in its thick, fleshy stems. And cacti don't grow thin leaves that might dry out quickly in the sunshine.

urface are always pulled by articles underneath. This ension creates a "skin" on water hat can support tiny insects.

Why can't I breathe

Fish can breathe underwater because they have gills, which let water in and out, and filter oxygen from it. But you have lungs, which

Why do I float better in seawater?

Seawater contains lots of salt, so it is denser than the water in a swimming pool or lake and can support more of your weight.

underwater?

only breathe air. If you
tried to breathe like a
fish, you would drown.

Why do people wear goggles?
If you like to keep your eyes open
underwater, goggles can protect
them from chlorine and salt,
which can sting. They
also help you see
more clearly.